Praises to Hymn

Meditations on Beloved Hymns and Carols

To Hymn Series

By John L. Hoh, Jr.

ISBN: 978-1-365-44666-5

HoneyMilk Publishing
An imprint of H2O Scrolls & Codices
North Prairie Wisconsin

Table of Contents

John L Hoh Jr

CHRISTMAS

98 Of the Father's Love Begotten

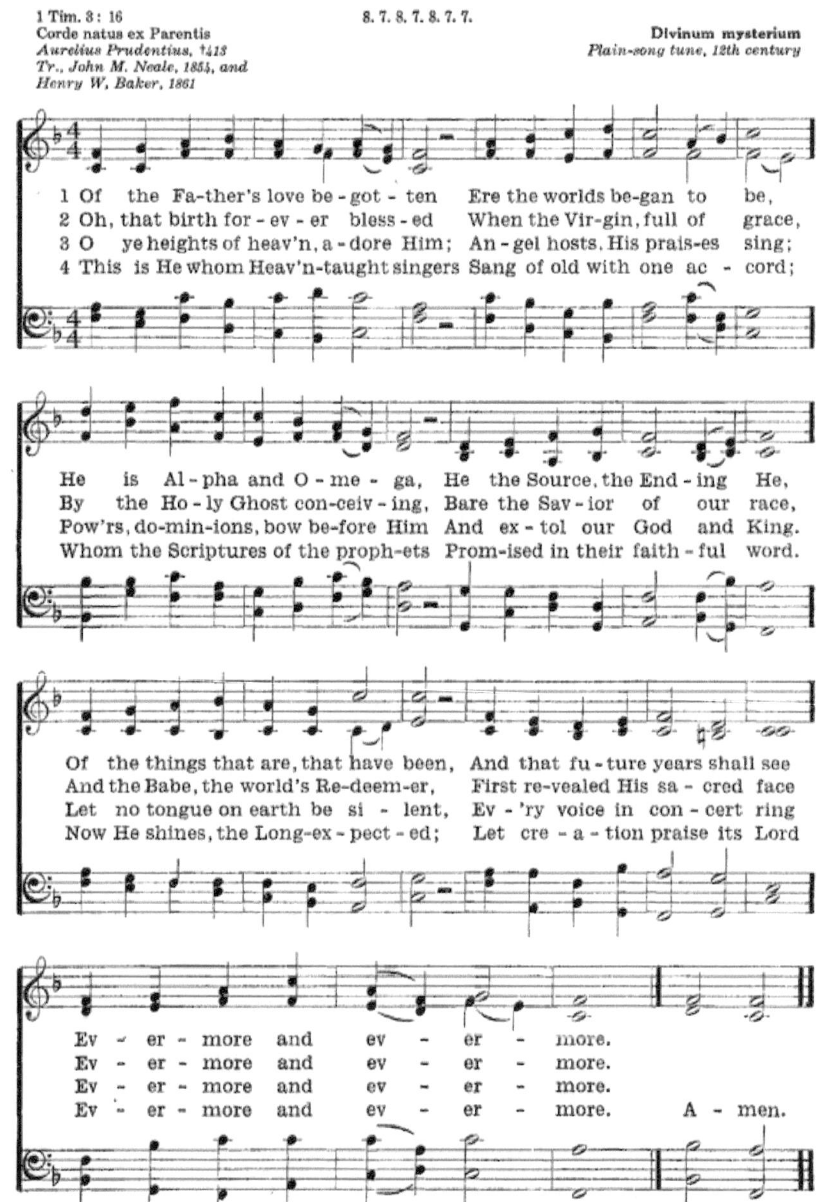

Of The Father's Love Begotten

“Of The Father's Love Begotten” is a hymn that comes down to us from Prudentius in the 5th Century. Christians have been singing it for over 1500 years.

Aurelius Clemens Prudentius was born in 348AD in Spain. A Christian Latin poet, Prudentius wrote a number of hymns, occasional Christian lyrics, and poems on saints. Although he held a high place at the Roman court, he eventually retired to devote himself to religion.

Prudentius has been called “the father of Christian allegory.” Prudentius achieved distinction in government administration but retired in later life to write devotional poetry, becoming the first to use the classical Latin verse forms with complete success in the service of the new faith. His lyrical poetry includes Hymns for the Day, a cycle of twelve hymns for various times of the day, parts of which are still found in modern hymnals; and Crowns of Martyrdom, fourteen long poems celebrating the lives of martyrs, including “The Passion of Agnes.” Prudentius also wrote two long didactic poems: *Apotheosis*, on the doctrine of the Trinity; and *Hamartigenia* (Origin of Sin), which attacks the Gnostic theologian Marcion. Other works include *Psychomachia*, an allegorical description of the struggle between (Christian) virtues and (pagan) vices; *Contra Symmachum*, a polemic against paganism based on the events of the year 384; and a series of 49 poems describing biblical scenes depicted in wall paintings on a Roman church--a valuable source on Christian iconography.

The date of the hymn's writing, though not entirely known, can be deduced through the life of Prudentius. Prudentius would have lived at the time of the Arian heresy and the Council at Nicea. The hymn reflects many of the statements set out in the Athanasian Creed.

A look at the theology of this hymn reflects the unique nature of Christ as reflected in this hymn.

The hymn has become a standard Christmas hymn in the church, usually in association with John 1:1-18.

Of the Father's Love Begotten

by Aurelius C. Prudentius, 413, cento Translated by John. M. Neale, 1818-1866 and Henry W. Baker, 1821-1977

1. *Of the Father's love begotten*
Ere the worlds began to be,
He is Alpha and Omega,
He the Source, the Ending He,
Of the things that are, that have been,
And that future years shall see
Evermore and evermore.

The hymn starts straight off on why a small baby was born in Bethlehem. There was a cosmic quality to this birth, an eternal element, an ingredient that defies reason and logic. “Of the Father’s love begotten.” God so love the world that he gave his one and only Son that whoever believes in him should not perish but have everlasting life (John 3:16). And this begetting occurred before the world was created! The joyful message of Christmas is this: God knew what all people would do before he created the world and us people in it. He knew what each of us would do before he created each one of us. Yet he still created the world, and he still sent His Son to die for us. No matter what you did, you are forgiven through the blood of Christ.

Prudentius reminds us of the words spoken to John in his Revelation: Jesus is the Alpha and Omega. Jesus was there at the earth's creation. You know what that means? Jesus was in consultation with his Father in creating the people who would rebel! Jesus knew, creating those people, that he would have to die to pay for their sins!

And in the end, Jesus will be ruling, just as he rules now from on high.

2. *Oh, that birth forever blessed*
   When the Virgin, full of grace,
   By the Holy Ghost conceiving,
   Bare the Savior of our race,
   And the Babe, the world's Redeemer,
   First revealed His sacred face
   Evermore and evermore.

Prudentius now takes us to that manger in Bethlehem. Look, the virgin has conceived and has given birth—and has called him name Immanuel ("God with us)!

Notice how Prudentius describes Mary? "Full of grace." It was by grace that Mary was chosen to be the vessel of God, not because she was sinless. In her "Magnificat", Mary states her sinful condition when she states "because of God my Savior." She states her need of a Savior and, paradoxically, that she is bearing and giving birth to that Savior!

3. *O ye heights of heaven, adore Him;*
   Angel hosts, His praises sing;
   Powers, dominions, bow before Him

And extol our God and King.
Let no tongue on earth be silent,
Every voice in concert ring
Evermore and evermore.

Can't you just see that angelic choir singing above Judea's hillsides to the shepherds? Prudentius sums up that scene eloquently in this verse, stating the totality of the heavenly chorus.

And, of course, the shepherds couldn't keep this news to themselves. They rushed to see the baby, then rushed to announce the joyous news. No doubt the citizens of Bethlehem were all astir on that night so long ago, the Roman legions standing guard on alert. Just what were they to make of this spectacle?

4. *This is He whom Heaven-taught singers*
   Sang of old with one accord;
   Whom the Scriptures of the prophets
   Promised in their faithful word.
   Now He shines, the Long-expected;
   Let creation praise its Lord
   Evermore and evermore.

Lest we think the angels were out of place, Prudentius tells us that the angels stated the fulfillment of Old Testament prophets. Taking a cue from St. Paul ("If anyone, even an angel, speaks a Gospel different than the Gospel I proclaimed to you, let him be condemned" Galatians 1:8), Prudentius points out the angelic message's harmony with Old Testament prophesy.

5. *Christ, to Thee, with God the Father,*
   And, O Holy Ghost, to Thee
   Hymn and chant and high thanksgiving
   And unending praises be,
   Honor, glory, and dominion,

And eternal victory
Evermore and evermore.

Prudentius finishes (in this English version found in *The Lutheran Hymnal*) with a Trinitarian doxology, common among early Christians. It reasserts the truths of the Trinity stated in the Athanasian Creed as well as the honor due the Triune God, which includes the Son of God, the baby lying in Bethlehem's manger.

Source of lyrics:

The Lutheran Hymnal

Hymn #98

Text: 1 Tim. 3:16

Author: Aurelius C. Prudentius, 413, cento Translated by: John. M. Neale, 1854 and Henry W. Baker, 1861

Titled: "Corde natus ex Parentis"

Tune: "Divinum mysterium", Plain-song tune, 12th century

DE EVCHARISTIA.

XXXVIII.

Diuinum mysteri um

modò declaratur, & mens infidelium

tumens

tumens execratur, firma spe credentium

fides robora tur.

Panis primo cernitur, qui dùm consecratur,
Christus tunc porrigitur, & sub pane datur,
Quomodo efficitur, Christus operatur.

Et vinum similiter cum sit benedictum
Et tunc est veraciter sanguis Christi dictum:
Credimus communiter verum est non fictum.

Fides est summoperè credere in Deum,
Panem sanctum edere & tractare eum,
Iubet Christus sumere, Hoc est corpus meum.

Nobis celebrantibus istud Sacramentum,
Et cunctis credentibus fiat nutrimentum:
Iudæis negantibus fit in detrimentum.

Pater, Nate, Spiritus almum consolamen
Det nobis propitius nostrum restauramen,
Vt cum cœli ciuibus personemus, Amen.

Iesus

The original Latin, for all you Latin scholars:

Corde natus ex parentis

1. corde natus ex parentis ante mundi exordium
   A et O cognominatus, ipse fons et clausula omnium quae sunt, fuerunt, quaeque post futura sunt.

2. Ipse iussit et creata, dixit ipse et facta sunt, terra, caelum, fossa ponti, trina rerum machina,
   quaeque in his vigent sub alto solis et lunae globo.

3. Corporis formam caduci, membra morti obnoxia induit, ne gens periret primoplasti ex germine,
   merserat quem lex profundo noxialis tartaro.

4. O beatus ortus ille, virgo cum puerpera edidit nostram salutem, feta Sancto Spiritu, et puer redemptor orbis os sacratum protulit.

5. Psallat altitudo caeli, psallite omnes angeli, quidquid est virtutis usquam psallat in laudem Dei,
   nulla linguarum silescat, vox et omnis consonet.

6. Ecce, quem vates vetustis concinebant saeculis, quem prophetarum fideles paginae spoponderant, emicat promissus olim; cuncta conlaudent eum.

7. Macte iudex mortuorum, macte rex viventium, dexter in Parentis arce qui cluis virtutibus, omnium venturus inde iustus ultor criminum.

8. Te senes et te iuventus, parvulorum te chorus,
   turba matrum, virginumque, simplices puellulae,
   voce concordes pudicis perstrepant concentibus.

9. Tibi, Christe, sit cum Patre hagioque Pneumate
   hymnus, decus, laus perennis, gratiarum actio,
   honor, virtus, victoria, regnum aeternaliter.

CHRISTMAS

85 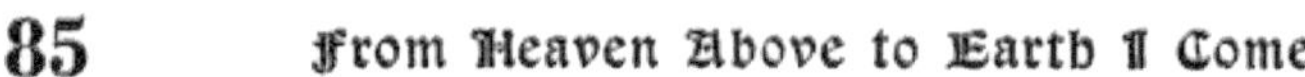

Luke 2: 1-18 L. M.
Vom Himmel hoch, da komm' ich her
Martin Luther, 1535
Tr., Catherine Winkworth, 1855, alt.

Vom Himmel hoch
"Geistliche Lieder"
Leipzig, 1539

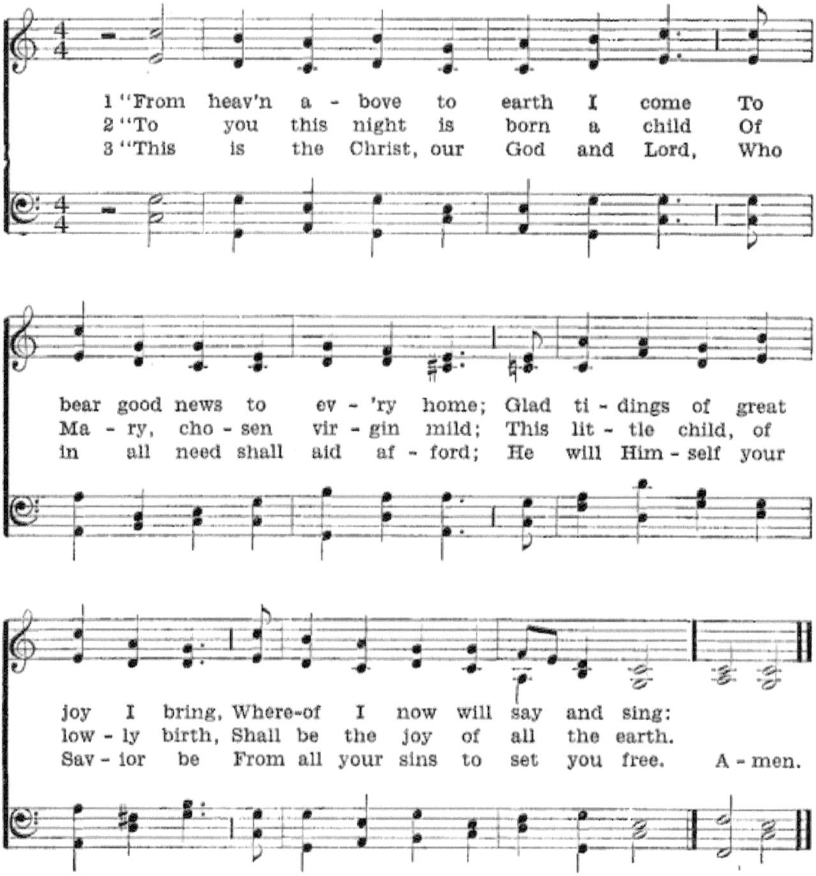

1 "From heav'n a - bove to earth I come To
2 "To you this night is born a child Of
3 "This is the Christ, our God and Lord, Who

bear good news to ev - 'ry home; Glad ti - dings of great
Ma - ry, cho - sen vir - gin mild; This lit - tle child, of
in all need shall aid af - ford; He will Him - self your

joy I bring, Where-of I now will say and sing:
low - ly birth, Shall be the joy of all the earth.
Sav - ior be From all your sins to set you free. A - men.

4 "He will on you the gifts bestow
Prepared by God for all below,
That in His kingdom, bright and fair,
You may with us His glory share.

5 "These are the tokens ye shall mark:
The swaddling-clothes and manger dark;
There ye shall find the Infant laid
By whom the heavens and earth were made."

From Heaven Above to Earth I Come

Hymn 85 from The Lutheran Hymnal

Text: Luke 2: 1-18

Author: Martin Luther, 1535

Tune: Vom Himmel hoch, da komm' ich her

Translated by: Catherine Winkworth, 1855, alt.

1st published in: "Geistliche Lieder" Leipzig, 1539

Luther had a little tradition with his household (and likely included students who couldn't make it to their homes for Christmas). This hymn he wrote would be sung in two parts; the first verses sung by someone dressed like an angel and descending a staircase, while the last verses were sung by the assemble household members at the bottom of the staircase.

Luther had a childlike appreciation for Christmas. Read Roland Bainton's Luther's Christmas Book for more on Luther and Christmas.

The "angel" sang:

1. "From heaven above to earth I come
   To bear good news to every home;
   Glad tidings of great joy I bring,
   Whereof I now will say and sing:

2. "To you this night is born a child
   Of Mary, chosen virgin mild;
   This little child, of lowly birth,
   Shall be the joy of all the earth.

3. "This is the Christ, our God and Lord,
   Who in all need shall aid afford;
   He will Himself your Savior be
   From all your sins to set you free.

4. "He will on you the gifts bestow
   Prepared by God for all below,
   That in His kingdom, bright and fair,
   You may with us His glory share.

5. "These are the tokens ye shall mark:
   The swaddling-clothes and manger dark;
   There ye shall find the Infant laid
   By whom the heavens and earth were made."

The assembly would sing:

6. Now let us all with gladsome cheer
   Go with the shepherds and draw near
   To see the precious gift of God,
   Who hath His own dear Son bestowed.

7. Give heed, my heart, lift up thine eyes!
   What is it in yon manger lies?
   Who is this child, so young and fair?
   The blessed Christ-child lieth there.

8. Welcome to earth, Thou noble Guest,
Through whom the sinful world is blest!
Thou com'st to share my misery;
What thanks shall I return to Thee?

9. Ah, Lord, who hast created all,
How weak art Thou, how poor and small,
That Thou dost choose Thine infant bed
Where humble cattle lately fed!

10. Were earth a thousand times as fair,
Beset with gold and jewels rare,
It yet were far too poor to be
A narrow cradle, Lord, for Thee.

11. For velvets soft and silken stuff
Thou hast but hay and straw so rough,
Whereon Thou, King, so rich and great,
As 'twere Thy heaven, art throned in state.

12. And thus, dear Lord, it pleaseth Thee
To make this truth quite plain to me,
That all the world's wealth, honor, might,
Are naught and worthless in Thy sight.

13. Ah, dearest Jesus, holy Child,
Make Thee a bed, soft, undefiled,
Within my heart, that it may be
A quiet chamber kept for Thee.

14. My heart for very joy doth leap,
My lips no more can silence keep;
I, too, must sing with joyful tongue
That sweetest ancient cradle-song:

15. Glory to God in highest heaven,
Who unto us His Son hath given!
While angels sing with pious mirth
A glad new year to all the earth.

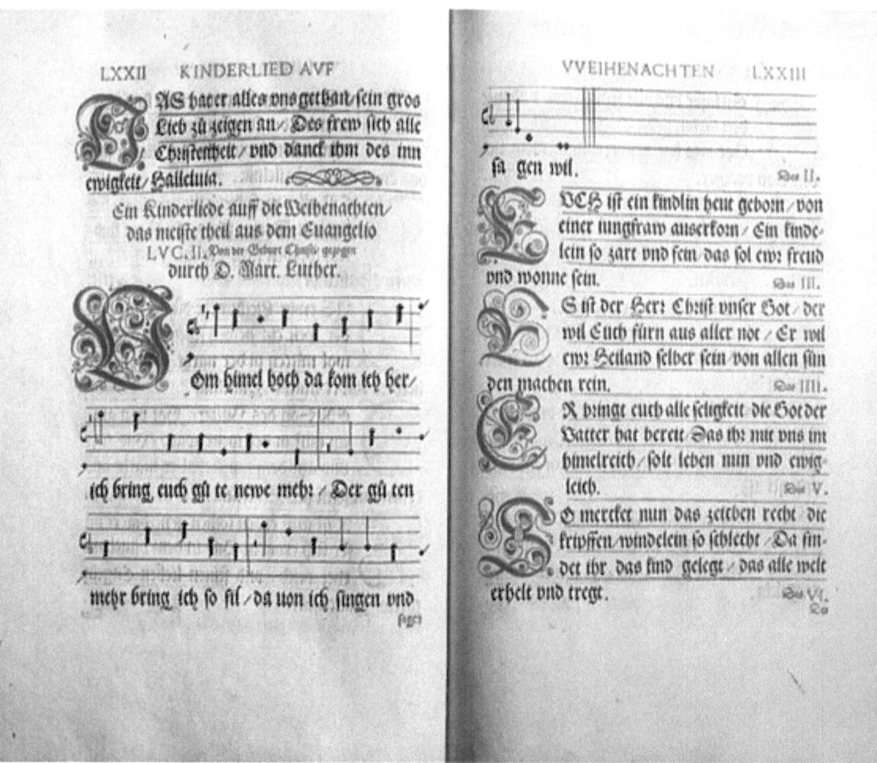

LXXII KINDERLIED AVF

DAS hat er alles uns gethan/ sein gros Lieb zu zeigen an/ Des frew sich alle Christenheit/ und danck ihm des inn ewigkeit/ Halleluia.

Ein Kinderliede auff die Weihenachten/ das meiste theil aus dem Euangelio LVC. II. Von der Geburt Christi gezogen durch D. Mart. Luther.

VVEIHENACHTEN LXXIII

Das II.

EUCH ist ein kindlin heut geborn/ von einer iungfraw auserkorn/ Ein kindelein so zart und fein/ das sol ewr freud und wonne sein.

Das III.

ES ist der Herr Christ unser Got/ der wil Euch fürn aus aller not/ Er wil ewr Heiland selber sein/ von allen sünden machen rein.

Das IIII.

ER bringt euch alle seligkeit/ die Got der Vatter hat bereit/ Das ihr mit uns im himelreich/ solt leben nun und ewigleich.

Das V.

SO merket nun das zeichen recht/ die krippen/ windelein so schlecht/ Da findet ihr das kind gelegt/ das alle welt erhelt und tregt.

Das VI.

	"Vom Himmel hoch, da komm ich her" (German)	*Translation by Catherine Winkworth (1855)*
1	Vom Himmel hoch, da komm ich her. Ich bring' euch gute neue Mär, Der guten Mär bring ich so viel, Davon ich singn und sagen will.	From heaven above to earth I come To bear good news to every home; Glad tidings of great joy I bring Whereof I now will say and sing:
2	Euch ist ein Kindlein heut' geborn Von einer Jungfrau auserkorn, Ein Kindelein, so zart und fein, Das soll eu'r Freud und Wonne sein.	To you this night is born a child Of Mary, chosen mother mild; This little child, of lowly birth, Shall be the joy of all your earth.
3	Es ist der Herr Christ, unser Gott, Der will euch führn aus aller Not, Er will eu'r Heiland selber sein, Von allen Sünden machen rein.	'Tis Christ our God who far on high Hath heard your sad and bitter cry; Himself will your Salvation be, Himself from sin will make you free.
4	Er bringt euch alle Seligkeit, Die Gott der Vater hat bereit, Daß ihr mit uns im Himmelreich Sollt leben nun und ewiglich.	He brings those blessings, long ago Prepared by God for all below; Henceforth His kingdom open stands To you, as to the angel bands.
5	So merket nun das Zeichen recht: Die Krippe, Windelein so schlecht, Da findet ihr das Kind gelegt, Das alle Welt erhält und trägt.	These are the tokens ye shall mark, The swaddling clothes and manger dark; There shall ye find the young child laid, By whom the heavens and earth were made.
6	Des laßt uns alle frölich sein Und mit den Hirten gehn hinein, Zu sehn, was Gott uns hat beschert, Mit seinem lieben Sohn verehrt.	Now let us all with gladsome cheer Follow the shepherds, and draw near To see this wondrous gift of God Who hath His only Son bestowed.
7	Merk auf, mein Herz, und sieh dorthin! Was liegt dort in dem Krippelein? Wes ist das schöne Kindelein? Es ist das liebe Jesulein.	Give heed, my heart, lift up thine eyes! Who is it in yon manger lies? Who is this child so young and fair? The blessed Christ-child lieth there.
8	Sei mir willkommen, edler Gast! Den Sünder nicht verschmähet hast Und kommst ins Elend her zu mir, Wie soll ich immer danken dir?	Welcome to earth, Thou noble guest, Through whom e'en wicked men are blest! Thou com'st to share our misery, What can we render, Lord, to Thee!
9	Ach, Herr, du Schöpfer aller Ding, Wie bist du worden so gering, Daß du da liegst auf dürrem Gras, Davon ein Rind und Esel aß!	Ah, Lord, who hast created all, How hast Thou made Thee weak and small, That Thou must choose Thy infant bed Where ass and ox but lately fed!

	"Vom Himmel hoch, da komm ich her" (German)	*Translation by Catherine Winkworth (1855)*
10	Und wär' die Welt vielmal so weit, Von Edelstein und Gold bereit', So wär sie doch dir viel zu klein, Zu sein ein enges Wiegelein.	Were earth a thousand times as fair, Beset with gold and jewels rare, She yet were far too poor to be A narrow cradle, Lord, for Thee.
11	Der Sammet und die Seide dein, Das ist grob Heu und Windelein, Darauf du König groß und reich Herprangst, als wär's dein Himmelreich.	For velvets soft and silken stuff Thou hast but hay and straw so rough, Whereon Thou King, so rich and great, As 'twere Thy heaven, art throned in state.
12	Das hat also gefallen dir, Die Wahrheit anzuzeigen mir: Wie aller Welt Macht, Ehr und Gut Vor dir nichts gilt, nichts hilft noch tut.	Thus hath it pleased Thee to make plain The truth to us poor fools and vain, That this world's honour, wealth and might Are nought and worthless in Thy sight.
13	Ach, mein herzliebes Jesulein, Mach dir ein rein, sanft Bettelein, Zu ruhen in meins Herzens Schrein, Das ich nimmer vergesse dein.	Ah! dearest Jesus, Holy Child, Make Thee a bed, soft, undefiled, Within my heart, that it may be A quiet chamber kept for Thee.
14	Davon ich allzeit fröhlich sei, Zu springen, singen immer frei Das rechte Susaninne schon, Mit Herzenslust den süßen Ton.	My heart for very joy doth leap, My lips no more can silence keep; I too must sing with joyful tongue That sweetest ancient cradle-song.
15	Lob, Ehr sei Gott im höchsten Thron, Der uns schenkt seinen ein'gen Sohn. Des freuen sich der Engel Schar Und singen uns solch neues Jahr.	Glory to God in highest heaven, Who unto man His Son hath given! While angels sing with pious mirth A glad New Year to all the earth.

94 Hark! the Herald Angels Sing

7. 7. 7. 7. D., with Refrain

Luke 2: 14
Charles Wesley, 1739, et al.

Mendelssohn
Felix Mendelssohn, 1840, ad.

Hark! The Herald Angels Sing

Felix Mendelssohn contributed to music both secular and to the church. The tune for "Hark! The Herald Angels Sing" was from Mendelssohn's own repertoire. But how the tune came to be married to the carol is another story. And on top of this story is the story of how we got "Hark! The Herald Angels Sing."

"Hark! The Herald Angels Sing" was written by Charles Wesley in 1737. Originally he called it "Hark, how all the welkin rings, Glory to the King of Kings!" Welkin is an old English word that means "heaven," "sky," or "the vaults of heaven."

The words we have today came from George Whitefield, an old college friend of Wesley's. Friendship, however, has its limits. Wesley did not like the change in lyrics. It was his contention that the Scriptures do not speak of angels singing in Luke's account (although the King James Version does have "a multitude of the heavenly host," unless Wesley believed there were more entities than angels in that heavenly choir). The carol hymn was popular before; it became even more popular with the change. Wesley steadfastly refused to sing the new words, although that's fair. He did write the carol hymn, after all.

But Mendelssohn's tune still wasn't part of the "Hark!" hymn. I haven't found anyone anywhere who knows what the actual tune (or tunes) originally sung with this hymn were. Whatever tune or tunes were used became lost in the mists of history as Mendelssohn's tune became the popular tune fixed in the public mind.

The tune used, named "Mendelssohn," was not originally intended for any Christmas carol or hymn, much less this one. In fact it wasn't intended for church use. In 1855 William Cummings took Mendelssohn's "Festgesang an die Knustler" and matched it up with Whitefield's words. "Festgesang" was a tribute to Johann Gutenberg and his invention of the movable type printing press. Today this combination is considered a Christmas classic and featured in almost all hymnals and a majority of Christmas albums.

Note: I'm not sure when the refrain was added—whether it was added by George Whitefield or added to fit Mendelssohn's tune.

George Whitefield's words	Charles Wesley's words
1. Hark! The herald angels sing, "Glory to the newborn King; Peace on earth, and mercy mild, God and sinners reconciled!" Joyful, all ye nations rise, Join the triumph of the skies; With th'angelic host proclaim, "Christ is born in Bethlehem!"	1. Hark, how all the welkin rings, "Glory to the King of kings; Peace on earth, and mercy mild, God and sinners reconciled!" 2. Joyful, all ye nations, rise, Join the triumph of the skies; Universal nature say, "Christ the Lord is born to-day!"
Refrain Hark! the herald angels sing, "Glory to the newborn King!"	
2. Christ, by highest heav'n adored; Christ the everlasting Lord; Late in time, behold Him come, Offspring of a virgin's womb.	3. Christ, by highest Heaven ador'd, Christ, the everlasting Lord: Late in time behold him come, Offspring of a Virgin's womb!

George Whitefield's words	Charles Wesley's words
Veiled in flesh the Godhead see; Hail th'incarnate Deity, Pleased with us in flesh to dwell, Jesus our Emmanuel.	4. Veiled in flesh, the Godhead see, Hail the incarnate deity! Pleased as man with men to appear, Jesus! Our Immanuel here!
Refrain Hark! the herald angels sing, "Glory to the newborn King!"	
3. Hail the heav'nly Prince of Peace! Hail the Sun of Righteousness! Light and life to all He brings, Ris'n with healing in His wings.	5. Hail, the heavenly Prince of Peace! Hail, the Sun of Righteousness! Light and life to all he brings, Risen with healing in his wings.
Mild He lays His glory by, Born that man no more may die. Born to raise the sons of earth, Born to give them second birth.	6. Mild He lays his glory by, Born that man no more may die; Born to raise the sons of earth; Born to give them second birth.
Refrain Hark! the herald angels sing, "Glory to the newborn King!"	
4. Come, Desire of nations, come, Fix in us Thy humble home; Rise, the woman's conqu'ring Seed, Bruise in us the serpent's head.	7. Come, Desire of nations, come, Fix in us thy humble home; Rise, the woman's conquering seed, Bruise in us the serpent's head.
Now display Thy saving power, Ruined nature now restore; Now in mystic union join Thine to ours, and ours to Thine.	8. Now display thy saving power, Ruined nature now restore; Now in mystic union join Thine to ours, and ours to thine.
Refrain Hark! the herald angels sing, "Glory to the newborn King!"	

<table>
<tr><th>George Whitefield’s words</th><th>Charles Wesley’s words</th></tr>
<tr><td rowspan="2">5. Adam’s likeness, Lord, efface,
Stamp Thine image in its place:
Second Adam from above,
Reinstate us in Thy love.
Let us Thee, though lost, regain,
Thee, the Life, the inner man:
O, to all Thyself impart,
Formed in each believing heart.</td><td>9. Adam’s likeness, Lord, efface;
Stamp Thy image in its place.
Second Adam from above,
Reinstate us in thy love.</td></tr>
<tr><td>10. Let us Thee, though lost, regain,
Thee, the life, the inner Man:
O! to all thyself impart,
Form’d in each believing heart.</td></tr>
<tr><td>Refrain
Hark! the herald angels sing,
“Glory to the newborn King!”</td><td></td></tr>
</table>

467 Built on the Rock the Church doth Stand

Eph. 2: 19-22
Kirken den er et gammelt Hus
Nicolai F. S. Grundtvig, 1837
Tr., Carl Döving, 1909, alt.

8. 8. 8. 8. 8. 8. 8.

Kirken den er et
Ludvig M. Lindeman, 1871

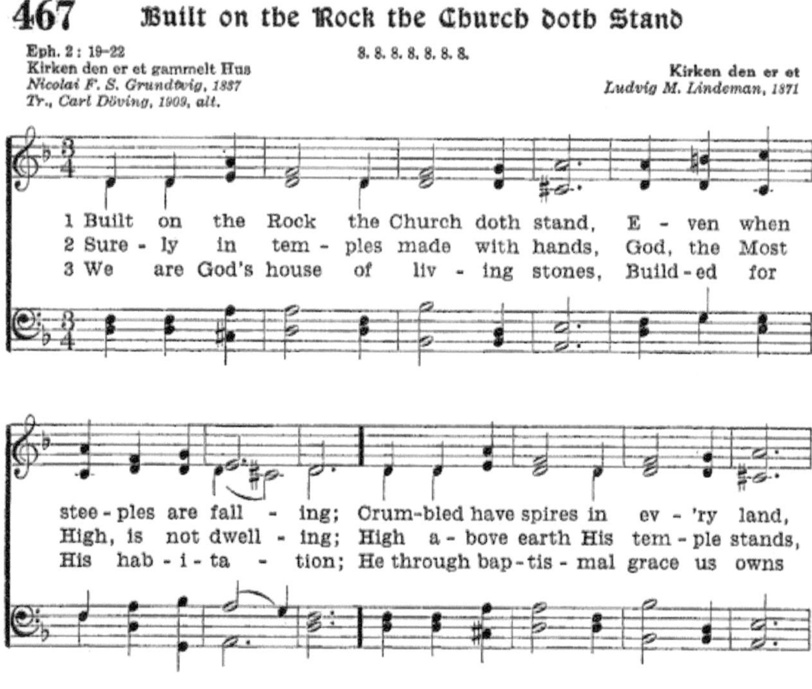

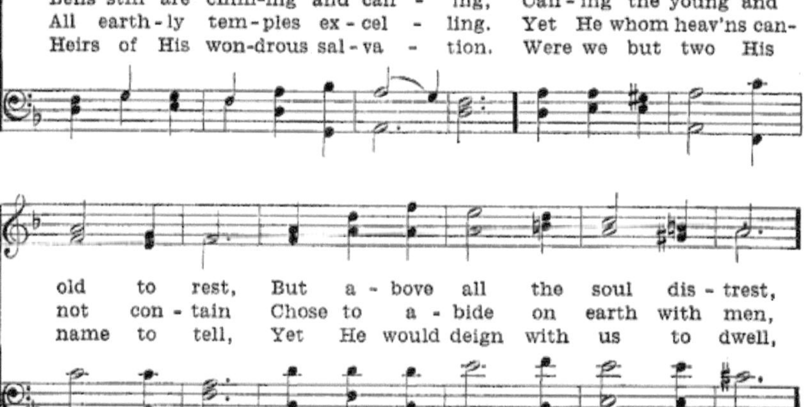

Built on the Rock the Church Doth Stand

One of my favorite hymns in *The Lutheran Hymnal* (TLH) is “Built on the Rock the Church doth Stand.” Written by Nicolai Grundtvig in 1837, it paints a vivid picture of the "holy, Christian and apostolic Church"—what we call the Invisible Church in confirmation class. This hymn, number 467 in *TLH* (132, *Lutheran Hymnary*), is appropriately placed among the Communion of Saints hymns. Read the hymn and you will see a clear exposition of the teaching of the invisible Church.

Nicolai Grundtvig did have his warts. The early history of the Norwegian Synod (today's Evangelical Lutheran Synod) reveals that early Norwegian immigrants brought with them the “Grundtvigian error.” The Grundtvigian error, simply put, placed the Apostles' Creed as inspired and thus equal to Scripture. Fortunately, this error was detected very early in Norwegian Synod history and corrected. Just as fortunate is that Grundtvig wrote such a fine hymn that has been preserved for us.

The hymn begins “Built on the Rock the Church doth stand, Even when steeples are falling.” We can see the timeless truth and beauty in this phrase. Our faith and our salvation are not based on a church building. It is based on the Rock of faith—the Rock to which Jesus refers in Matthew

16:18. The Church (invisible) is based on faith in Christ Jesus and his atonement for all of our sins. Yes, steeples will fall. My home congregation decommissioned its old church building in 1977—but that congregation still thrives! The temple in Jerusalem was destroyed by Nebuchadnezzar in the Old Testament, yet God's people still worshiped him "by the rivers of Babylon" (Psalm 137). Paul proclaimed the Good News in synagogues, by the riverbanks, in prison, and even in the public debates and in court. The true Church is found where there are those who believe, not necessarily where the tallest steeples stand.

The next line is a chiastic parallel to the first. A chiastic parallel reverses the thoughts of the first line in the second line. Here, we have the parallelism in "Crumbled have spires in every land, Bells still are chiming and calling." Again, the visible church building does not make Christians—faith in Christ does!

Who do these bells "chime and call?" It calls "the young and old to rest." It first and foremost "calls the soul distrest (distressed), the soul which is longing for rest everlasting." There, in the Church of Christ, the Christian aching and hurting from sin finds comfort. It finds comfort in the Gospel message that tells us that yes, indeed, our sins are all forgiven! What comfort we can take! It is the Word of God upon which we base our hope. It is the Gospel message of the Word becoming flesh and dwelling among us, dying on the cross in our place to pay for our sins.

Built on the Rock the Church doth stand,
Even when steeples are falling;
Crumbled have spires in every land,
Bells still are chiming and calling,
Calling the young and old to rest,
But above all the soul distrest,
Longing for rest everlasting.

TLH 467, v. 1 (Hymnary 132, v. 1)

Where do we find God? Mankind throughout earth's dreary history have attempted to answer that question. The Greeks looked to Mount Olympus. Nations saw gods manifested in their rulers. Nature religions would have us believe that God is all around in everything we see. The New Age movement tells us that we are all gods.

Yet we are left with an emptiness. We still recognize our sinfulness. We know that we are not perfect. We still seek that God who must be appeased for our many sins.

In seeking God mankind has erected temples. Yet in many temples godlessness took over. Drunkenness and prostitution became the norm in a great majority of these temples. Obviously God will not be found where his will is severely scorned.

The Old Testament Jews felt that God lived in their temple. This attitude carried over into Jesus' day. Because of this attitude, many Jews felt that God would preserve Jerusalem—simply because the temple was in Jerusalem!

But God has no need for “temples made with hands.” “High above earth his temple stands.” When Jesus spoke with the Samaritan woman at Jacob's well, he told her exactly what God wished. She wanted to know if Jerusalem was indeed the true worship site or if Mount Gerizim, where the Samaritans traditionally worshiped, was adequate. Jesus answered:

> *“Believe me, woman, a time is coming when you will worship the Father neither on this mountain nor in Jerusalem. You Samaritans worship what you do not know; we worship what we do know, for salvation is from the Jews. Yet a time is coming and has now come when the true worshipers will worship the Father in spirit and truth, for they are the kind of worshipers the Father seeks. God is spirit, and his worshipers must worship in spirit and in truth.” (John 4:21-24)*

Grundtvig, though, reminds us that God is contained neither in any earthly temple nor in heaven. God also dwells on earth. He dwelt in the person of Jesus Christ. But most importantly he dwells in our hearts. Our bodies, God's own unique little creations, are the hallowed temples of God. The Almighty God who could choose any place on earth or in heaven to dwell chose to dwell instead in—our frail "clay jars!"

What an honor to host the Ruler of heaven and earth each and every day that we live! Though we don't deserve such an honor, it is an honor which our Father seeks us out in order to give us. How our lives take on a whole new meaning. We are no longer lowly mud hovels or straw huts. We are palaces of the King of kings and Lord of lords! We may not feel like royal palaces. That is because we are going through remodeling each and every day of our lives. The Holy Spirit does this remodeling. These temples would be worthless on their own merits. But God has bought your temple and mine; he has seen fit to dwell in us; he continually remodels us until we are perfected in heaven. Live in joy as God's holy temple!

Surely in temples made with hands,
God, the most high, is not dwelling;
High above earth His temple stands,
All earthly temples excelling.
Yet He whom heav'ns cannot contain
Chose to abide on earth with men,
Built in our bodies his temple.

TLH 467, verse 2 (Hymnary 132, verse 2)

Saint Peter writes and reminds us of who we are:

> *"You also, like living stones, are being built into a spiritual house to be a holy priesthood, offering spiritual sacrifices acceptable to God through Jesus Christ." (1 Peter 2:5)*

As living stones Peter also reminds us that our cornerstone is Christ Jesus, whom the Jewish leaders as well as natural man has rejected—but chosen personally by God the Father!

God chooses all Christians as "living stones" for his habitation. He has purchased each of us "through baptismal grace." He purchased us to make us "Heirs of His wondrous salvation." Through his innocent and precious blood God has purchased each of us. In our baptism God seals us as His own.

What requirements must be met in order to be a valid stone? Is there a quota of "stones" necessary? Must they be a certain shape? The early Christian church had in its midst a book entitled *The Shepherd of Hermas*. In this book Hermas receives the vision of a Tower (the Church) under construction. There are many stones in the tower, many more lying around and still more that were tossed far away from the building. These stones all represented various types of believers who came into contact with the Church. Yet the only ones that fit into the tower's construction were those that were a certain size and shape. The other stones could not be used unless they were modified. Even then they could not be a part of the Tower. Instead, they would be placed inside the tower.

How contrary to Scripture this is! Peter, though denying Christ, still was a "living stone" in the Church. Paul was a persecutor of the Church and also was a "living stone." Despite the deep cracks and fissures left by sin, God still picks us up, washes us off, fills in the cracks with his forgiveness and sets us in his church.

Saint Matthew records for us the words of Jesus when Jesus says:

> *"For where two or three come together in my name, there am I with them." (Matthew 18:20)*

How beautifully Grundtvig expresses this in his hymn: "Were we but two his name to tell, Yet He would deign with us to dwell, With all His grace and favor." How comforting that God's grace and presence does not rely on numbers! Even for the sake of ten righteous people God was willing to spare Sodom and Gomorrah. Think of the percentage that would have been—yet God was willing to spare those two cities for the sake of that minority (Genesis 19)! A remnant of Israel would return to Palestine, Jesus would send out twelve apostles to proclaim his Gospel. Gideon would fight and conquer the Midianites with a mere three hundred men (Judges 7). As the Lord said to Paul:

> *"My grace is sufficient for you, for my power is made perfect in weakness." (2 Corinthians 12:9).*

God's "weaknesses" are greater than any power. With little God can accomplish much.

You and I are temples of God. We are placed as "living stones" in God's church. We may see our talents as insignificant. Yet with these talents and gifts God has equipped each of us for his work.

> *We are God's house of living stones,*
> *Builded for His habitation;*
> *He through baptismal grace us owns*
> *Heirs of His wondrous salvation.*
> *Were we but two His name to tell*
> *Yet He would deign with us to dwell,*
> *With all His grace and His favor.*

TLH 467, verse 3 (Hymnary 132, verse 3)

"Hello. My name is John Hoh. I'm from Good Shepherd Lutheran Church here in Kalispel. We meet on Sundays at the Outlaw Inn in the Hideout Room."

With this introduction, or one similar to it, I canvassed the city of Kalispel, Montana, in the summer of 1988. The Hideout Room was a rather small, basement conference room that received little use in the Outlaw Inn. In one corner was a wet bar, something that was less than a favorable impression to visitors. The chalkboard that I used to try to hide the bar was less than totally adequate.

Yet there in that setting the Gospel was proclaimed. We even had visitors that normally wouldn't have known about confessional Lutheranism or hadn't planned on attending church on a Sunday during vacation. They came because we were right in the hotel and they wouldn't have to travel anywhere and try to find another church. Indeed God works in mysterious ways!

Anyone who has had any contact with home missions or mission groups realize the truth in the fourth verse penned by Grundtvig: "Now we may gather with our King E'en in the lowliest dwelling." Having also served on Travel/Canvass/Witness expeditions in the Wisconsin Evangelical Lutheran Synod (WELS) I have also worshiped with fellow Christians in schools, a Senior Citizens' bridge club building, and in a YMCA. Others have worshiped in mortuaries, homes, and restaurants. Does it matter where we worship? No, for God is present among his people and his means of grace are dispensed within the fellowship of believers. Often such a setting induces some to come who would normally be intimidated in a normal church setting. Again, the power of God is at work.

Yet how often do we share the opinion of King David? King David wanted to build a temple for God. He felt that it was undignified that God's house was a tent! Yet God reminded David what his plan was. Solomon would build the temple. David would build the dynasty from which the King of kings and Savior of the world would come (1 Chronicles 28:1-7). More important than the physical building is the spiritual habitat. God seeks to live in our hearts, not in a grand cathedral. He wishes to live with us, not apart from us tucked away in a pristine chapel.

How many kings do you know would gather in humble surroundings? Yet the King of kings, our Almighty God, does just that. He remains with us here on earth. He is with us every step of our lives. He resides within our hearts. Indeed, he came as a lowly baby, born to poor parents. He was literally "born in a barn." He learned a carpenter's trade. Indeed our King is also our High Priest who gave himself as the sacrifice for all our sins. This priestly king found it necessary to dwell among men. The writer to the Hebrews tells us:

> *"We do not have a high priest who is unable to sympathize with our weaknesses, but we have one who has been tempted in every way, just as we are--yet was without sin. (Hebrews 4:15).*

God thus comes to us, just as we are: broken, cast down, burdened with sin. He lifts us up, cleanses us and mends us through the blood shed on the cross. This message of forgiveness hallows the place where we worship him. It is this Truth which makes a house God's home.

> *Now we may gather with our King*
> *E'en in the lowliest dwelling;*
> *Praises to Him we there may bring,*
> *His wondrous mercy forthtelling.*
> *Jesus His grace to us accords;*
> *Spirit and life are all His Words;*
> *His truth doth hallow the temple.*

TLH 467, verse 4 (Hymnary 132, verse 4)

Did you know that of all the major religions of the world only Christianity has no rules or guidelines for the construction of worship facilities? And of all the religions, Christians build the most elaborate and ornate structures for the worship of their Savior? It is amazing what God's grace leads men to do; even more amazing that a Christian wishes to show his or her praise in such a grand manner.

The goal of any mission group, either foreign or home, is to one day dedicate its own worship facility. It is not required that such a building be constructed. Yet it is a way for a group of Christians, called a congregation, to gather around the Word and Sacraments and to reach out to the community. It sends the signal: "Just as our God and Savior is with us, so we will remain here to do his work."

These temples are as varied as the people God has called to be his own. Some are built with brick; others with stone. There are white wooden structures and the Little Brown Church in the Vale. Some are built of corrugated metal; others with adobe. In the United States they may have majestic steeples rising up to heaven. In Russia we are familiar with the "onion domes." Some have bells, others carillons, while a few may even sport a glockenspiel. Some churches even have histories, such as the Evangelical Lutheran Synod church in Kennesaw, Georgia, that served as a hospital during the Civil War!

If the church building is merely constructed for show, it does not serve a useful purpose. The structure is to be a place where sinners gather to be convicted by the Law and to be forgiven in the Gospel. The church is not a "museum for saints but a hospital for sinners" as Ann Landers once wrote.

In the church Christ gathers all his believers—even the children. Unless we ourselves have faith like a child, we do not enter the kingdom of heaven no matter how many times we enter God's house in our midst. Beautiful things are said in these churches: We are saved by God's free grace, without cost to us! We are washed clean in the blood of the Lamb!

We are made God's children in baptism and strengthened in his Supper! God reveals the covenant he has made with us.

As natural rebels against God, we did not deserve any mercy. God was not obligated to make any covenant or to strike any bargain with us. As rebels we deserved nothing but death.

But through Christ God has made a covenant with us. It is the covenant made with Abraham. It is the covenant repeated through Moses and the prophets. This covenant was sealed in the perfect life and innocent death of his Son. This covenant declares us innocent of all charges. Our debt and punishment were placed on Christ's shoulders. Our Lord himself paid the price for all our sins.

Let us now herald his praises in whatever earthly temple we gather in, whether brick, wood, mud or steel. Whether in a church building, motel conference room, YMCA, mortuary or even in a fellow Christian's home. God is with us wherever we are and wherever we worship.

Still we our earthly temples rear
That we may herald His praises;
They are the homes where He draws near
And little children embraces.
Beautiful things in them are said;
God there with us His covenant made,
Making us heirs of His kingdom.

TLH 467, verse 5 (Hymnary 132, verse 5)

What, exactly, does our worship center on? What is the focus of our worship? 1993 marked the 75th. anniversary of the Evangelical Lutheran Synod. For this anniversary a set of nine paintings were commissioned. The first painting displays the bedrock of our faith—the Means of Grace.

The Means of Grace form the basis for the sixth verse of Grundtvig's hymn. As we stand in the church where we worship we can see the focal points that Grundtvig points out. Let us then look at these focal points of faith.

"Here stands the font before our eyes Telling how God did receive us." Maybe you yourself worship in a church where the font is in the entrance to the sanctuary. It is through baptism that we enter the Kingdom of God. Through baptism God seals us as his own children. As Jesus said to Nicodemus:

> *"Unless a man is born of water and the Spirit, he cannot enter the kingdom of God." (John 3:5).*

Here with water and the Word the Holy Spirit creates faith in the suckling babe. Here the water flows on the converted sinner making him or her God's own child. The presence of the font reminds us of Luther's words:

> ***What does baptizing with water mean?***
>
> *It means that our old Adam with his evil deeds and desires should be drowned by daily contrition and repentance, and die, and that day by day a new man should arise, as from the dead, to live in the presence of God in righteousness and purity now and forever.*

Luther also reminds us that "we ought not to say that we were baptized but that we are baptized." Baptism is continuous in our lives.

"The altar recalls Christ's sacrifice And what His table doth give us." A price must be paid for all our sins. The Old Testament Jews were led to sacrifice sheep and goats. Canaanite tribes offered children. The Indians of South America offered virgins as sacrifices to appease the gods. Yet the altar tells us that a sacrifice has been made on our behalf. This sacrifice was offered by none other than God himself! He now offers us grace, pardon and peace through his body and blood given to us through the communion of Lord's Supper.

In these sacraments we see the visible elements of God's power. Yet what makes these elements valid? What gives power to these elements? It is the Word of God.

As we look at the lectern and at the pulpit the Word of God is proclaimed to each one of us. The Law hands down its harsh judgment upon woeful sinners. It lays the souls of all men bare, showing each and every one of us that in God's sight we are all worthy of eternal death. The Word also lays out for us the Gospel. Though it is the opposite of the Law, it is also God's Word. But, as Luther says, "It is the higher word." The Gospel offers us peace and pardon. It tells us that we are all bought with a price. It is our comfort in distress, salve for troubled souls and guide as we pass from this world to the next.

Through these Means of Grace we are made God's own children and preserved in the one true faith to life everlasting. God changes not; neither does his Gospel promise. It is valid today as it was yesterday and will be tomorrow. God is our Redeemer!

Here stands the font before our eyes
Telling how God did receive us;
The altar recalls Christ's sacrifice
And what His table doth give us;
Here sounds the Word that doth proclaim
Christ yesterday, today, the same,
Yea, and for aye our Redeemer.

TLH 467, verse 6 (Hymnary 132, verse 6)

> *"All authority in heaven and on earth has been given to me. Therefore go and make disciples of all nations, baptizing them in the name of the Father and of the Son and of the Holy Spirit, and teaching them to obey everything I have commanded you. And surely I will be with you always, to the very end of the age (Matthew 28:18-20).*

With these words our Lord sent forth his disciples into the world. He sends us also with the same saving Gospel message to proclaim. Our reason for existing as congregations and synods is to publicly proclaim the Gospel of our Lord, administer the faith-giving and faith-strengthening sacraments and meet in fellowship with fellow Christians.

Our prayer is the same as the prayer with which Nicolai Grundtvig ended his hymn. The prayer is that many come to know that the price for their sins has been paid in full. May our churches' bells call many to come before the Lord. May these bells invite all sinners into God's kingdom.

You and I are those self-same church bells. In our words we share the message with our children and spouses and friends about the sacrifice Christ has made. Our lives reflect the life of the one who redeemed us and made us his own. Our worship gives thanks and praise to the one who created us, preserves us and saves us. We live guided by the one who has called, gathered and enlightened each of us as saints in the Church.

The one who has saved us by paying the awesome price for our sin is Jesus Christ, the Good Shepherd. The Good Shepherd definitely knows his sheep. His sheep recognize his voice. It is his voice which calms and soothes us with the comforting Gospel message.

Jesus also tells us that there are other sheep not yet of his flock. These he also seeks to save. He searches out these sheep as well. This seeking will continue until the Lord returns to judge.

Finally, this fine hymn concludes with a message of comfort: "My peace I leave with you." We need to realize that this isn't some unattainable earthly peace. Jesus himself tells us that because of him there would be strife, even in families! His disciples weren't given false delusions about their lot as apostles. Jesus warned them that they would suffer just as he suffered.

The peace which Christ leaves with us is peace with God. No longer do our sins separate us from our heavenly Father. Because of Christ's full and complete atonement we are now reconciled with God. We are redeemed from sin's bondage! We are adopted as children of God! We can confess with Saint Paul:

> *"I consider that our present sufferings are not worth comparing with the glory that will be revealed in us." (Romans 8:18).*

Freely we are given pardon and peace in the blood of Christ. Truly we have been made children of God. You and I will share joy and bliss with our God forever. To that we can join Nicolai Grundtvig is saying "Amen," that is "truth" or as Luther says, "Yea, yea, so shall it be." As Saint Paul says:

> *"Here is a trustworthy saying that deserves full acceptance: Christ Jesus came into the world to save sinners--of whom I am the worst." (1 Timothy 1:15).*

> *Grant, then, O God, where'er men roam,*
> *That, when the church bells are ringing,*
> *Many in saving faith may come*
> *Where Christ His message is bringing:*
> *"I know Mine own, Mine own know Me;*
> *Ye, not the world, My face shall see.*
> *My peace I leave with you." Amen.*

TLH 467, verse 7 (Hymnary 132, verse 7)

Original Norwegian:

1. Kirken den er et gammelt hus,
står, om end tårnene falde,
tårne fuldmange sank i grus,
klokker end kime og kalde,
kalde på gammel og på ung,
mest dog på sjælen træt og tung,
syg for den evige hvile.

2. Herren vor Gud vist ej bebor
huse, som hænder mon bygge,
arke-paulunet var på jord
kun af hans tempel en skygge.
Dog sig en bolig underfuld
bygged han selv af støv og muld,
rejste af gruset i nåde.

3. Vi er hans hus og kirke nu,
bygget af levende stene,
som, under kors, med ærlig hu
troen og dåben forene.
Var vi på jord ej mer end to,
bygge dog ville han og bo
hos os i hele sin vælde.

4. Samles vi kan da med vor drot
selv i den laveste hytte,
finde med Peder: der er godt,
tog ej al verden i bytte.
Kirken og vi, som ærlig tro,
altid er et så vel som to, -
et med vor drot og hinanden!

5. Husene dog med kirke-navn,
bygte til Frelserens ære,
hvor han de små tog tit i favn,
er os som hjemmet så kære.
Dejlige ting i dem er sagt,
sluttet har der med os sin pagt
han, som os Himmerig skænker.

6. Fonten os minder om vor dåb,
altret om nadverens glæde,
hvor skulle før i tro og håb
Herren vi finde til stede,
end hvor det for os prentet står:
Herren i dag er som i går,
så er og troen og dåben.

7. Give da Gud, at hvor vi bo,
altid, når klokkerne ringe,
folket forsamles i Jesu tro
dér, hvor det plejed at klinge:
Verden vel ej, men I mig ser,
alt hvad jeg siger, se, det sker,
fred være med eder alle!

8. Aldrig dog glemmes mer i Nord
kirken af levende stene,
dem, som i kraften af Guds ord
troen og dåben forene!
Selv bygger Ånden kirke bedst,
trænger så lidt til drot som præst,
ordet kun helliger huset!

36 Now Thank We All Our God

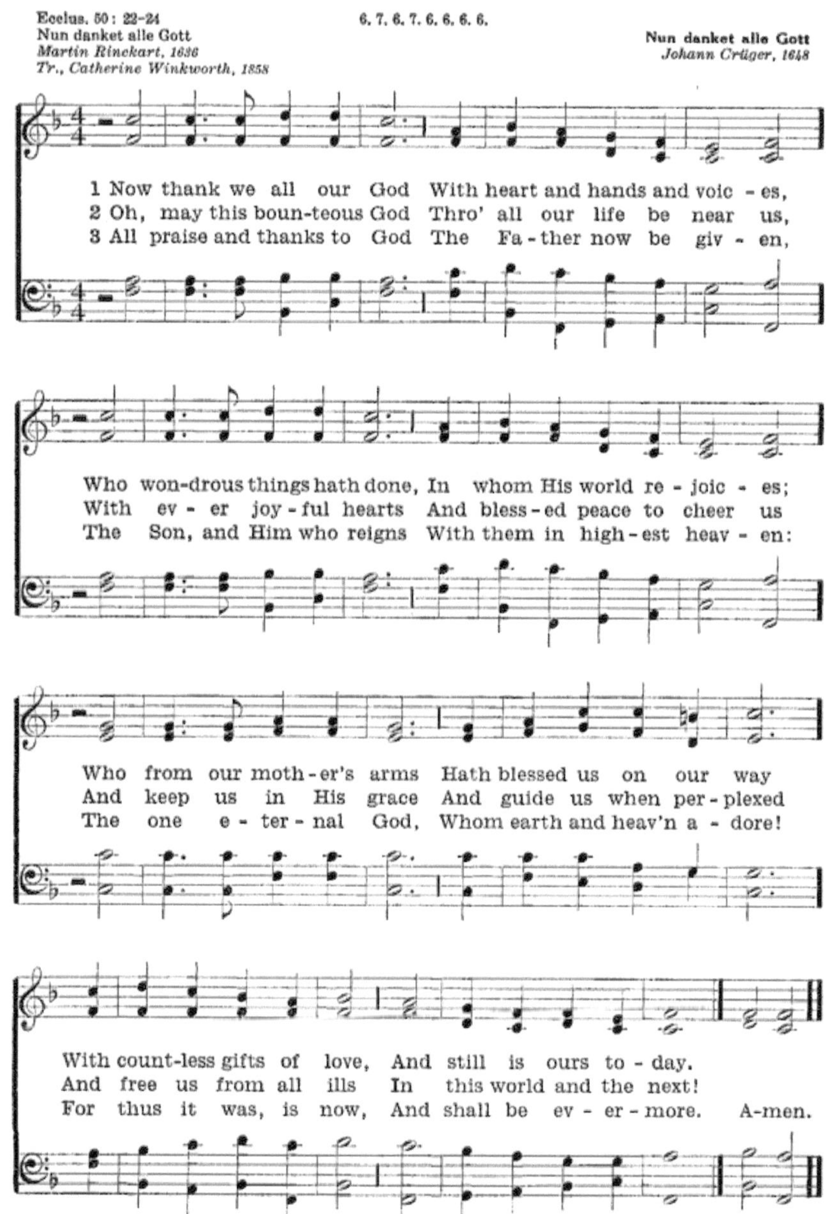

Now Thank We All Our God

Martin Rinkart was a pastor in the little city of Eilenberg in Saxony during the Thirty Years' War. This walled city was the goal of refugees during that time. They came and ate all the food, and then there was starvation. With the starvation came pestilence, until practically the whole population of the city died. Martin Rinkart, the only pastor left in the city, had as many as fifty funerals in one day. One evening after having conducted funerals all day, he sank down exhausted, thinking that he could bear it no longer; but then it was he wrote the words of the famous hymn:

> *Now thank we all our God*
> *With heart and hands and voices,*
> *Who wondrous things hath done,*
> *In whom His world rejoices;*
> *Who, from our mothers' arms*
> *Hath blessed us on our way*
> *With countless gifts of love,*
> *And still is ours today.*

Luther wrote:

"Yes, it is the will of God for us that we give thanks. If we were not thankful we would go insane with the perplexities and irregularities of life's experiences. If there was ever a time when we needed to be thankful it is in the hour of crisis; because if we are not thankful, we will be overwhelmed by despair."

More than one hymn writer has drawn inspiration, as well as, in some cases, the words themselves, from the Apocrypha. For example, the exalted hymn of thanksgiving, "Nun danket alle Gott," written by Pastor Martin Rinkart about 1636 when the devastating Thirty Years War was nearing its end, is dependent upon Luther's translation of Sirach 50:22-24. Two stanzas of the hymn, as translated by Catherine Winkworth, will show the amount of borrowing (here printed in italics):

Now thank we all our God
With heart and hands and voices,
Who wondrous things hath done,
In whom His world rejoices;
Who, from our mother's arms,
Hath blessed us on our way
With countless gifts of love,
And still is ours today.

O may this bounteous God
Through all our life be near us,
With ever joyful hearts
And blessed peace to cheer us;
And keep us in His grace,
And guide us when perplexed,
And free us from all ills
In this world and the next.

John L Hoh Jr

F C F B F Dm
1. Nun dan - ket al - le Gott mit
der gro - ße Din - ge tut an
Gm Dm Eb F C F C
Her - zen, Mund und Hän - den,
uns und al - len En - den,
der
Gm C Am D Gm B6 Am G4 3
uns von Mut - ter - leib und Kin - des - bei - nen
C F B F Gm D
an un - zäh - lig viel zu-
Gm F/A B6 C4 3 F
gut und noch jetz - und ge - tan.

Original German *Liedtext*:

1 Nun danket alle Gott
mit Herzen, Mund und Händen,
der große Dinge tut
an uns und allen Enden,
der uns von Mutterleib
und Kindesbeinen an
unzählig viel zugut
und noch jetzund getan.

2 Der ewigreiche Gott
woll uns bei unserm Leben
ein immer fröhlich Herz
und edlen Frieden geben
und uns in seiner Gnad
erhalten fort und fort
und uns aus aller Not
erlösen hier und dort.

3 Lob, Ehr und Preis sei Gott,
dem Vater und dem Sohne
und dem, der beiden gleich
im höchsten Himmelsthrone,
dem dreimal einen Gott,
wie es ursprünglich war
und ist und bleiben wird
jetzund und immerdar.

388 Just as I Am, without One Plea

John 6: 37 — L. M. — St. Crispin

Charlotte Elliott, 1836 — *(FIRST TUNE)* — George J. Elvey, 1862

2 Just as I am and waiting not
To rid my soul of one dark blot,
To Thee, whose blood can cleanse each spot,
O Lamb of God, I come, I come.

3 Just as I am, though tossed about
With many a conflict, many a doubt,
Fightings and fears within, without,
O Lamb of God, I come, I come.

4 Just as I am, poor, wretched, blind;
Sight, riches, healing of the mind,
Yea, all I need, in Thee to find,
O Lamb of God, I come, I come.

5 Just as I am, Thou wilt receive,
Wilt welcome, pardon, cleanse, relieve;
Because Thy promise I believe,
O Lamb of God, I come, I come.

6 Just as I am; Thy love unknown
Has broken every barrier down.
Now to be Thine, yea, Thine alone,
O Lamb of God, I come, I come.

Just as I am

Lutheran hymnody is rich in history, variety, and doctrine. It is the musical catechism! With hymns Lutherans have expressed, taught, and learned their faith.

An important lesson, which "Just as I Am" teaches, is that Jesus comes to us and seeks us out "just as we are." The epistle writer said it best when he wrote, "While we were yet sinners Christ died for us."

Often when I canvass or make evangelism calls, people say, "Oh, I'm not ready for the Lord yet. There's too much in my life I need to fix up." People in our recovery program, when they relapse, avoid coming to church. When they return, we welcome them with open arms and seek to assist them in their on-going recovery. There is a principle and a doctrine at work here. It is God who created us and it is God who creates faith in our hearts. It is also God who creates a new life within us here on earth and re-creates us for eternal life!

Please read the following piece on how "Just as I Am" was written.

> *An elderly man asked Charlotte Elliott if she were a Christian; she felt insulted, and told him to mind his own affairs. But after the man left, she could not get the question off her mind, and she went back to ask the man*

how to find Christ. He told her to come just as she was. She did, and wrote the beautiful song, "Just As I Am." - By B. A. Scherr

JUST AS I AM By Charlotte Elliott

1. *Just as I am, without one plea,*
   But that Thy blood was shed for me,
   And that Thou bidst me come to Thee,
   O Lamb of God, I come, I come.
2. *Just as I am, and waiting not*
   To rid my soul of one dark blot,
   To Thee whose blood can cleanse each spot,
   O Lamb of God, I come, I come.
3. *Just as I am, though tossed about*
   With many a conflict, many a doubt,
   Fightings and fears within, without,
   O Lamb of God, I come, I come.
4. *Just as I am, poor, wretched, blind;*
   Sight, riches, healing of the mind,
   Yea, all I need in Thee to find,
   O Lamb of God, I come, I come.
5. *Just as I am, Thou wilt receive,*
   Wilt welcome, pardon, cleanse, relieve;
   Because Thy promise I believe,
   O Lamb of God, I come, I come.
6. *Just as I am, Thy love unknown*
   Hath broken every barrier down;
   Now, to be Thine, yea, Thine alone,
   O Lamb of God, I come, I come.
7. *Just as I am, of that free love*
   The breadth, length, depth, and height to prove,
   Here for a season, then above,
   O Lamb of God, I come, I come!

Source: Signs of the Times, Copyright (c) July 26, 1942, Pacific Press

John L Hoh Jr

44 Ye Lands, to the Lord Make a Jubilant Noise

Ps. 100
Al Verden nu raabe for Herren med Fryd
Ulrik V. Koren, 1874
Tr., Harriet R. Spaeth, 1899, alt.

11. 5. 11. 9.

Guds Menighed, syng
Erik Hoff, c. 1860

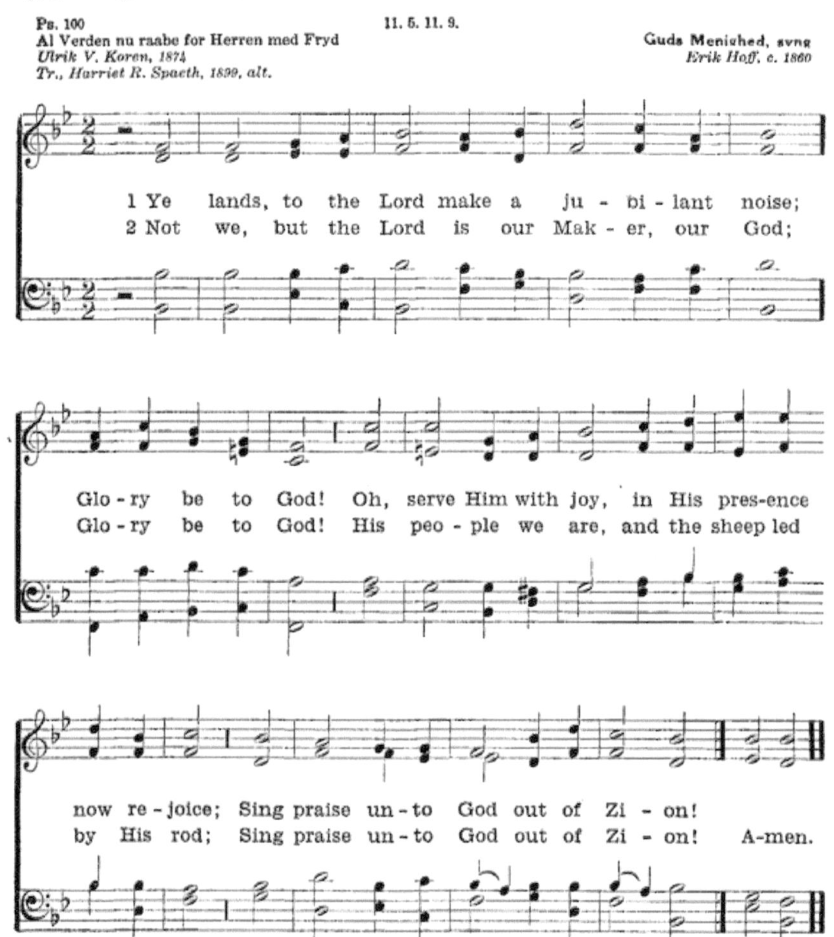

3 Oh, enter His gates with thanksgiving and praise;
Glory be to God!
To bless Him and thank Him our voices we will raise;
Sing praise unto God out of Zion!

4 For good is the Lord, and His mercy is sure;
Glory be to God!
To all generations His truth shall still endure;
Sing praise unto God out of Zion!

Ye Lands, to the Lord Make a Jubilant Noise

Many hymns in Lutheran hymnals express thanksgiving to God. And well Lutherans should be thankful. We are saved by grace through faith! We are God's own dear children! For this all Christians can be thankful.

One hymn that expresses thanks is one written by a Norwegian Lutheran pastor from Decorah, Iowa. It was my privilege to serve as vicar in two congregations he founded (among the over thirty he started in Iowa and Minnesota and Wisconsin).

Ulrik V. Koren's hymn is full of thanks and praise to God and calls on all creation to thank and praise God. This hymn was written even though Koren pastored over 30 churches, founded Luther College in Decorah, Iowa, and was president of the Norwegian Synod of the Evangelical Lutheran Church in America.

The hymn's tune is not the German variety most Lutherans are used to. It has a feel of an antiphon that the congregation could sing back and forth. I'll set up a possible format for congregational singing of this hymn at the end.

Two refrains echo through each verse: “Glory be to God” and “Sing Praise unto God out of Zion.” Each phrase looks to God alone for blessings, providence, and salvation.

Have a Happy Thanksgiving, and “Sing Praise unto God out of Zion.”

"Ye Lands, to the Lord Make a Jubilant Noise" by Ulrik V. Koren, 1826-1910

Translated by Harriet R. Spaeth, 1845-1925

Text From: *The Handbook To The Lutheran Hymnal* (St. Louis: Concordia Publishing House, 1942) p.38-39

1. *Ye lands, to the Lord make a jubilant noise;*
   Glory be to God!
   Oh, serve Him with joy, in His presence now rejoice;
   Sing praise unto God out of Zion!
2. *Not we, but the Lord is our Maker, our God;*
   Glory be to God!
   His people we are, and the sheep led by His rod;
   Sing praise unto God out of Zion!
3. *Oh, enter His gates with thanksgiving and praise;*
   Glory be to God!
   To bless Him and thank Him our voices we will raise;
   Sing praise unto God out of Zion!
4. *For good is the Lord, and His mercy is sure;*
   Glory be to God!
   To all generations His truth shall still endure;
   Sing praise unto God out of Zion!

Congregational Setting #1

1. *Pastor: Ye lands, to the Lord make a jubilant noise;*
   Congregation: Glory be to God!
   Pastor: Oh, serve Him with joy, in His presence now rejoice;
   Congregation: Sing praise unto God out of Zion!

2. *Pastor: Not we, but the Lord is our Maker, our God;*
   Congregation: Glory be to God!
   Pastor: His people we are, and the sheep led by His rod;
   Congregation: Sing praise unto God out of Zion!

3. *Pastor: Oh, enter His gates with thanksgiving and praise;*
   Congregation: Glory be to God!
   Pastor: To bless Him and thank Him our voices we will raise;
   Congregation: Sing praise unto God out of Zion!

4. *Pastor: For good is the Lord, and His mercy is sure;*
   Congregation: Glory be to God!
   Pastor: To all generations His truth shall still endure;
   Congregation: Sing praise unto God out of Zion!

Congregational Setting #2

1. *Pastor: Ye lands, to the Lord make a jubilant noise;*
   Congregation: Glory be to God!
   Oh, serve Him with joy, in His presence now rejoice;
   Pastor: Sing praise unto God out of Zion!

2. *Pastor: Not we, but the Lord is our Maker, our God;*
   Congregation: Glory be to God!
   His people we are, and the sheep led by His rod;
   Pastor: Sing praise unto God out of Zion!

3. *Pastor: Oh, enter His gates with thanksgiving and praise;*
   Congregation: Glory be to God!
   To bless Him and thank Him our voices we will raise;
   Pastor: Sing praise unto God out of Zion!

4. *Pastor: For good is the Lord, and His mercy is sure;*
   Congregation: Glory be to God!
   To all generations His truth shall still endure;
   Pastor: Sing praise unto God out of Zion!

In both settings, you can exchange Pastor/Congregation with Left Side/Right Side, Choir/Congregation, or Pastor/Choir.

Notes from *The Lutheran Hymnal*

Hymn #44

Text: Ps. 100

Author: Ulrik V. Koren, 1874

Translated by: Harriet R. Spaeth, 1899, alt.

Titled: "Al Verden nu raabe for Herren med Fryd" Composer: Erik Hoff, c. 1860

Tune: "Guds Menighed, syng"

Original Norwegian:

Al verden nu raabe for Herren med Fryd,
Lovet være Gud!
Træd frem for hans ansigt med sang og jubellyd,
Guds menighed love nu Herren!

Kom, kjend Gud, din herre, du intet selv formaar,
Lovet være Gud!
Han, han har dig gjort til sit folk og fødes faar,
Guds menighed love nu Herren!

Gaar ind ad hams porte med lov og takkesang,
Lovet være Gud!
Velsigner, høilover evindelig hans navn,
Guds menighed love nu Herren!

Guds godhed og miskundhed er ny i evighed,
Lovet være Gud!
Fra slegt og til slegt skal hans sandhed vare ved,
Guds menighed love nu Herren!

On Eagles' Wings

Have you ever felt "down in the dumps?" Have things looked bleak at certain times in your life? Have you ever felt lower than a snake in a wagon rut and wish someone could lift you up?

We have all felt despair and hopelessness at times in our life. We may wonder where our next meal may come from, how we will pay that mountain of bills, look for a cure for our illness or infirmity, or just feel alone and have no one to turn to.

In *Christian Worship: A Lutheran Hymnal*, one can find a comforting hymn with a beautiful melody. Hymn #440, "On Eagles' Wings," capsulizes for Christians the providence and protection we receive from God. The refrain states:

> *And he will raise you up on eagles' wings,*
> *Bear you on the breath of dawn,*
> *Make you to shine like the sun,*
> *And hold you in the palm of his hand.*

The predominant themes in this refrain are found in Isaiah's prophecy. In Isaiah 40:31 we read:

> *...but those who hope in the* LORD

will renew their strength.

They will soar on wings like eagles;

In Isaiah 49:16 Isaiah writes:

"See, I have engraved you on the palms of my hands!"

Even in the midst of announcing judgment upon the nation of Judah, our God promised his people that He would protect them and be with them. They would have the strength of God's uplifting spirit, a strength equated with eagles' wings. Our God also assured his people of individual protection, just as someone would protect a frail bird or small pet in the palm of one's hand. This verse immediately follows God's rhetorical question:

Can a mother forget the baby at her breast
and have no compassion on the child she has borne?
Though she may forget, I will not forget you!

Although the phrase "bear you on the breath of dawn" is not found in Scripture, its meaning is found in the latter part of Isaiah 40:31:

"They will run and not grow weary, they will walk and not be faint."

The intent of the hymn verse is that God's Word refreshes us. Certainly the pressures of sin, Satan, and our flesh tire our soul. On our own we soon despair of the futility of our own righteousness--we either recognize that we can never appease God or we can never be sure we have done enough. Even hoping that we have done enough leaves us wondering, "Did I?" But the righteousness that comes from God refreshes us, just as sleep refreshes us and we awake in the morning renewed in our energy and zeal. At dawn we often feel as if we can run and not grow weary; walk and not grow faint.

The hymn writer's phrase, "Make you to shine like the sun," is a thought expressed by two writers in Holy Scripture. The judge, Deborah, sings at the conclusion of her victory song:

> *"So may all your enemies perish, O Lord! But may they who love you be like the sun when it rises in its strength."*
> *Judges 5:31*

Jesus echoes these sentiments in explaining the parable of the weeds to his disciples:

> *"Then the righteous will shine like the sun in the kingdom of their Father." Matthew 13:43*

In both passages, the believers are placed among the heathen and endure persecution. In both cases the persecution is allowed to continue in order that the believer may be "tested in the fire." But when the persecution has reached the limit God has placed on it, the believer will "shine like the sun." The believer's faith will be on full public display to the world, a faith that is a direct reflection of God's providence and mercy. It is a faith that shines because it trusts in God alone for full and free forgiveness in the blood of Christ.

To the Christian, the ultimate comfort comes from the blood- stained cross of Christ. Here on this splintered log edifice soaked red with blood stands testimony of God's love and providence for sinful people. Here we see our God in human flesh dying an agonizing death so that we all might have life—and have it to the full.

Once we see this cross with its willing victim giving up his life for our sins, then we can understand the investment God has made in us. And if God has given up his life to give us eternal life, then the trials and tribulations we face here on earth are bearable. We can joyfully live our lives in witness to the grace, mercy, and providence of God.

Ride as God lifts you up on eagles' wings; snuggle in the palm of his hand. God has made you his own dear child whom no one can snatch away from Him. In His blood you now shine like the sun.

656 Behold a Host, Arrayed in White
Rev. 7: 13-17
8. 8. 8. 6. 12 lines
Den store hvide Flok vi se
Hans A. Brorson, c. 1760
Tr., composite
Great White Host
Norwegian folk-tune c. 1600
Arr. by Edvard H. Grieg, †1907, ad.
1 Be-hold a host, ar-rayed in white, Like thousand snow-clad mountains bright,
2 Despised and scorned, they sojourned here; But now, how glo-rious they ap-pear!
3 Then hail, ye might-y le-gions, yea, All hail! Now safe and blest for aye,
With palms they stand. Who is this band Be - fore the throne of light?
Those mar-tyrs stand a priest-ly band, God's throne for-ev-er near.
And praise the Lord, who with His Word Sus-tained you on the way.
Lo, these are they of glo-rious fame Who from the great af - flic-tion came
So oft, in trou-bled days gone by, In an-guish they would weep and sigh.
Ye did the joys of earth dis-dain, Ye toiled and sowed in tears and pain.
And in the flood of Je - sus' blood Are cleansed from guilt and blame.
At home a-bove the God of Love For aye their tears shall dry.
Fare-well, now bring your sheaves and sing Sal - va - tion's glad re - frain.
Now gath-ered in the ho - ly place, Their voic-es they in wor-ship raise,
They now en-joy their Sab-bath rest, The pas-chal ban-quet of the blest;
Swing high your palms, lift up your song, Yea, make it myr-iad voic-es strong.

Behold A Host Arrayed in White

The church year draws to a close right after Thanksgiving. The Advent season kicks off a new Church year. Thus the Sundays of Pentecost draw to a close.

The final three Sundays of Pentecost are known as the Sundays of the End Times. In these weeks we look at what Scripture says about the coming end of the world, the last Judgment, and our eternal life as part of the Great White Host.

And well the end of the Church Year should focus on the End Times, for Pentecost observes our lives in Christ. And what other terminus does a life in Christ have other than anticipating his return, preparing for heaven, and living eternally with our Lord in heaven with his Father?

In celebrating the End Times, we are celebrating the coming of our King to gather us to heavenly mansions. Advent's focus on the coming King also has a taste of End Times in it. Good planning will prevent the focus of end times from dragging out to seven total weeks.

Within the End Times time frame in the Church Year is Reformation, when we celebrate that we have an inheritance that is ours through grace by faith alone. Thanksgiving, though a secular holiday, falls in the End Times period and reminds us to give thanks to God for his gift of salvation even as we await his coming, or him calling us home to eternal rest.

A favorite hymn of mine is “Behold a Host, Arrayed in White.” Based on the vision of Saint John in Revelation of the Great White Host in heaven, the hymn is a joyous celebration of the eternal life awaiting us in heaven. It is a hymn that will be sung at my funeral, if I die before the Lord's return.

During this time we can repeat the Easter greeting of the ancient Christians: “Allelujah! Christ has Risen! He has risen indeed! Allelulah!” Easter is a major componenet of the End Times, because if Christ did not rise, we are still in our sins and we have no hope after death. Christ's resurrection means that the End Times and the Judgment are not to be feared, but rather are, as Matthew quotes Jesus, “Like birth pains.” Any mother will tell you that the pain of childbirth is forgotten once the mother holds her child for the first time. Our travails here on earth will be forgotten amid the joys of heaven.

"Behold a Host, Arrayed in White" by Hans A. Brorson, 1694-1764

Text From: *The Lutheran Hymnal* (St. Louis: Concordia Publishing House, 1941)

1. *Behold a host, arrayed in white,*
   Like thousand snow-clad mountains bright,
   With palms they stand.
   Who is this band
   Before the throne of light?
   Lo, these are they of glorious fame
   Who from the great affliction came
   And in the flood of Jesus' blood
   Are cleansed from guilt and blame.

Now gathered in the holy place,
Their voices they in worship raise,
Their anthems swell where God doth dwell,
Mid angels' songs of praise.

2. *Despised and scorned, they sojourned here;*
But now, how glorious they must appear!
Those martyrs stand a priestly band,
God's throne forever near.
So oft, in troubled days gone by,
In anguish they would weep and sigh,
At home above the God of Love
For aye their tears shall dry.
They now enjoy their Sabbath rest,
The paschal banquet of the blest;
The Lamb, their Lord, at festal board
Himself is Host and Guest.

3. *Then hail, ye mighty legions, yea,*
All hail! Now safe and blest for aye,
And praise the Lord, who with His Word
Sustained you on the way.
Ye did the joys of earth disdain,
Ye toiled and sowed in tears and pain.
Farewell, now bring your sheaves and sing
Salvation's glad refrain.
Swing high your palms, lift up your song,
Yea, make it myriad voices strong,
Eternally shall praise to Thee,
God, and the Lamb belong.

Notes:

Hymn #656 from *The Lutheran Hymnal*

Text: Revelation 7:13-17

Author: Hans Adolf Brorson, c. 1760

Translated by: composite

Titled: "Den store hvide Flok vi se" Norwegian folk- tune, c. 1600

Tune: "Great White Host"

Arranged by: Edvard H. Grieg, 1907, ad.

Congregational Setting

Verse 1:

CONGREGATION: Behold a host, arrayed in white,
Like thousand snow-clad mountains bright,
With palms they stand. Who is this band
Before the throne of light?

CHOIR: Lo, these are they of glorious fame
Who from the great affliction came
And in the flood of Jesus' blood
Are cleansed from guilt and blame.
Now gathered in the holy place,
Their voices they in worship raise,
Their anthems swell where God doth dwell,
Mid angels' songs of praise.

Verse 2:

PASTOR: Despised and scorned, they sojourned here;
But now, how glorious they must appear!
Those martyrs stand a priestly band,
God's throne forever near.

So oft, in troubled days gone by,
In anguish they would weep and sigh,
At home above the God of Love
For aye their tears shall dry.
They now enjoy their Sabbath rest,
The paschal banquet of the blest;
The Lamb, their Lord, at festal board
Himself is Host and Guest.

Verse 3:

CONGREGATION: Then hail, ye mighty legions, yea, All hail!
Now safe and blest for aye,
And praise the Lord, who with His Word
Sustained you on the way.
Ye did the joys of earth disdain,
Ye toiled and sowed in tears and pain.
Farewell, now bring your sheaves and sing
Salvation's glad refrain.
Swing high your palms, lift up your song,
Yea, make it myriad voices strong,
Eternally shall praise to Thee,
God, and the Lamb belong.

Verse Three can be sung antiphonally.

571 Den store hvide flok vi se

Mel.: Nebelong 1881

Åb 7,9-17. Hans Adolph Brorson (1765).

Original Norwegian:

1 Den store hvide flok vi se
som tusind bjerge fuld' af sne,
med skov omkring
af palmesving,
for tronen, - hvo er de?
Det er den helteskare, som
af hin den store trængsel kom
og har sig to't i Lammets blod
til Himlens helligdom!
Der holde de nu kirkegang
med uophørlig jubelklang
i høje kor,
hvor Gud han bor
blandt alle engles sang.

2 Her gik de under stor foragt,
men se dem nu i deres pragt
for tronen stå
med kroner på,
i Himlens præstedragt!
Sandt er det, i så mangen nød
tit tårestrøm på kinder fłød,
men Gud har dem,
straks de kom hjem,
aftørret på sit skød.
Nu holde de og har til bedst'
hos ham en evig løvsalsfest,
og Lammet selv,
ved livets elv,
er både vært og gæst.

3 Til lykke, kæmpesamling, ja,
o, tusind fold til lykke da,

at du var her
så tro især
og slap så vel herfra!
Du har foragtet verdens trøst,
så lev nu evig vel, og høst,
hvad du har så't
med suk og gråd,
i tusind engles lyst!
Ophøj din røst, slå palmetakt
og sjung af himmelkraft og magt:
Pris være dig
evindelig,
vor Gud og Lammet, sagt!

77 LORD, KEEP US STEADFAST IN THY WORD.
Martin Luther. 1541.
(First Tune.)
WITTENBERG. L. M.
Tr. by Catherine Winkworth. 1862.
"Geistliche Lieder," Wittenberg. 1543.
♩=66. 1. Lord, keep us stead-fast in Thy Word: Curb those who fain by craft or sword
2. Lord Je - sus Christ, Thy pow'r make known; For Thou art Lord of lords a - lone:
3. O Com-fort - er, of price - less worth, Send peace and u - ni - ty on earth,
Would wrest the kingdom from Thy Son, And set at naught all He hath done.
De - fend Thy Chris-ten-dom, that we May ev - er - more sing praise to Thee.
Sup - port us in our fi - nal strife, And lead us out of death to life. A - men.
78 LORD, KEEP US STEADFAST IN THY WORD.
Martin Luther. 1541.
(Second Tune.)
MENDON. L. M.
Tr. Catherine Winkworth. 1862.
Arr. by Lowell Mason. 1832.
♩= 100. 1. Lord, keep us stead - fast in Thy Word: Curb those who fain by craft or sword
2. Lord Je - sus Christ, Thy pow'r make known; For Thou art Lord of lords a - lone·
3. O Com-fort - er, of price - less worth, Send peace and u - ni - ty on earth,
Would wrest the king-dom from Thy Son, And set at naught all He hath done.
De - fend Thy Chris-ten - dom, that we, May ev - er - more sing praise to Thee.
Sup - port us in our fi - nal strife, And lead us out of death to life. A - men.

Lord, Keep us Steadfast in Thy Word

Author: Martin Luther, hymnologist and theologian

1. Lord, keep us steadfast in Thy Word;
   Curb those who fain by craft and sword
   Would wrest the Kingdom from Thy Son
   And set at naught all He hath done.

2. Lord Jesus Christ, Thy power make known,
   For Thou art Lord of lords alone;
   Defend Thy Christendom that we
   May evermore sing praise to Thee.

3. O Comforter of priceless worth.
   Send peace and unity on earth.
   Support us in our final strife
   And lead us out of death to life.

John L Hoh Jr

im Leben, und ich werd bleiben allezeit im Haus des HErren eben, auf Erd in der Christlich'n Gemein, und nach dem Tode werd' ich seyn bey Christo meinem HErren. Wolfg. Mosel.

356.

Erhalt uns, HErr, bey deinem Wort, und steur [der Feinde Christi / des Pabsts und Türcken] Mord, die JEsum Christum, deinen Sohn, stürtzen wollen von seinem Thron.

2. Beweis dein' Macht, HErr JEsu Christ, der du ein HErr all'r Herren bist, beschirm' dein' arme Christenheit, daß sie dich lob' in Ewigkeit.

3. GOtt Heilger Geist, du Tröster werth, gib dein'm Volck einerley Sinn auf Erd; steh bey uns in der letzten Noth, g'leit uns ins Leben aus dem Tod.

4. Ach HErr! laß dir befohlen seyn die arm bedrängten Christen dein; bey vestem Glauben sie erhalt, und reiß sie aus der Feind' Gewalt.

5. Ihr' Anschläg, HErr, zunichte mach, laß sie treffen die böse Sach, und stürtz sie in die Grub' hinein, die sie machen den'n Christen dein.

6. So werden sie erkennen doch, daß du, uns'r HErr GOtt, lebest noch, und hilfst gewaltig deiner Schaar, die sich auf dich verlassen gar.

357. Der 67. Psalm.

Es woll' uns GOtt genädig seyn, und seinen Segen geben, sein Antlitz uns mit hellem Schein erleucht' zum ew'gen Leben, daß wir erkennen seine Werck, und was ihn liebt auf Erden, und JEsus Christus, Heil und Stärck, bekandt den Heyden werden, und sie zu GOtt bekehren!

2. So dancken, GOtt, und loben dich die Heyden überalle, und alle Welt die freue sich, und sing mit grossem Schalle, daß du auf Erden Richter bist, und läß'st die Sünd' nicht walten: dein Wort die Hut und Weide ist, die alles Volck erhalten, in rechter Bahn zu wallen.

3. Es dancke, GOtt, und lobe dich das Volck in guten Thaten, das Land bring' Frucht,

	German Text	English Translation
1	Erhalt uns, Herr, bei deinem Wort, Und steur' des Papsts und Türken Mord, Die Jesum Christum, deinen Sohn, Stürzen wollen von seinem Thron.	Preserve us, Lord, with your word, and control the murderous rage of the Pope and the Turks, who would want to cast down Jesus Christ, your son, From his throne.
2	Beweis dein Macht, Herr Jesu Christ, Der du Herr aller Herren bist; Beschirm dein arme Christenheit, Dass sie dich lob in Ewigkeit.	Show your might, Lord Jesus Christ, you who are the Lord of lords; protect your poor Christian people, so that they may praise you forever.
3	Gott Heilger Geist, du Tröster wert, Gib dein'm Volk einerlei Sinn auf Erd, Steh bei uns in der letzten Not! G'leit uns ins Leben aus dem Tod!	God, the holy spirit, you precious comforter, Give to your people unity of purpose on earth, Stand by us in our last agony! Lead us out of death into life!
4	Ihr Anschläg, Herr, zu nichte mach, Laß sie treffen die böse Sach, Und stürz sie in die Grub hinein, Die sie machen den Christen dein.	Lord, let their attacks come to naught, Let their evil cause be destroyed, And plunge them into the graves, they had made for Your Christians.
5	So werden sie erkennen doch, Daß du, unsr Herr Gott, lebest noch Und hilfst gewaltig deiner Schar, Die sich auf dich verlässet gar.	Thus they will come to recognize, That You, our Lord God, still lives And powerfully helps out Your flock, Which very much depends upon You.
6	Verleih uns Frieden gnädiglich, Herr Gott, zu unsern Zeiten; Es ist doch ja kein andrer nicht, Der für uns könnte streiten, Denn du, unser Gott, alleine.	Grant us peace, in your mercy, Lord God, in our time; there is indeed no one else can fight the fight for us except you alone, our God.
7	Gib unsern Fürst'n und aller Obrigkeit Fried und gut Regiment, Dass wir unter ihnen Ein geruh'g und stilles Leben führen mögen In aller Gottseligkeit und Ehrbarkeit. Amen.	Grant to our Princes and all those in authority peace and good government so that we among then may lead a calm and peaceful life in all godliness and honesty. Amen.

www.ingramcontent.com/pod-product-compliance
Ingram Content Group UK Ltd.
Pitfield, Milton Keynes, MK11 3LW, UK
UKHW041922190726
13854UKWH00003B/1398